Mommy & I,

Cooking with Jesus

RECIPES & DEVOTIONAL

To Melissa

D e n i s e   P a s s

& the Seeing Deep Ministries Team

Many blessings to you! ♡

(contributor + editor)

Requests for permission should be directed to Denise Pass at denisepass@denisepass.com.
Printed in the United States of America. First printing 2021.
ISBN: 978-0-578-89404-1

To order additional copies of this resource, order online at www.amazon.com or visit www.denisepass.com for more information.

Cover design by Tabatha Haines, Interior Design by Tabatha Haines and Denise Pass, artwork provided by Canva, photography provided by Amber Trementozzi of AMT Photography & Design.

Edited by Jennifer Elwood and Denise Pass.

Seeing Deep Ministries
www.seeingdeep.com

"And these words that I command you today shall be on your heart. You shall teach them diligently to your children, and shall talk of them when you sit in your house, and when you walk by the way, and when you lie down, and when you rise."

—Deuteronomy 6:6-7 (ESV)

DEDICATION

To our sweet Savior Who created all things and all people—thank you for the gift of life and the gift of creating. Whether it is in the kitchen, making crafts, or making memories, there is something special when we get to create with the special people in our lives with You at the center, LORD. You are so good to allow us to experience Your presence together!

To my guinea pigs, I mean, my special people, my precious family and friends, who have tested and tasted everything I have made in the kitchen over the years . . . sometimes with joy and glee and sometimes not (especially as I had to navigate special diets). To my children who discovered wonders in the kitchen together with me as we giggled and created homemade pretzels, fun cakes, and yummy creations of all kinds. Sometimes a mess, sometimes a recipe that flopped, and sometimes something scrumptious! But always something amazing to be learned about God and each other. I love you and thank God for you and can't wait to get back in the kitchen with you again soon! And to my darling husband who is willing to try my creations now that they are usually two scary words together—healthy dessert. Thank you for being my willing victim.

To the Seeing Deep team—what a joy to create with you! Thank you for joining me in this fun journey and another one of my wild ideas. I thank God for each one of you and for your willingness to share special moments with you and your children in the kitchen, too.

Our team dedicates this book first to the LORD for His salvation that set us free to love others well. We thank Him for the food and creativity He also provides, that we can share fellowship and His provision together. And we thank Him for bringing people in our lives to share it all with. God is the Giver of it all. May we cherish one another with the gifts He gives. May our kitchen be a refuge where the pains in this life are mingled with the joy of God's provision as we demonstrate our love and care by making something comforting and delicious in the kitchen.

To you special mommas and kiddos with the gift of another day—seize the moments you are given with your tribe! Cherish one another and make the most of it. Enjoy the simple blessings of this life that you get to share together . . . and always include Jesus and His precious Word. We pray that you will have as much fun creating these recipes as we did.

FORWARD

There is something about the kitchen that brings us home to feelings of belonging and safety. Nurturing happens there. And in each one of our souls is a desire for the simple things of life like homemade bread, mishaps in the kitchen . . . and laughter.

I am forever grateful for memories of my mom baking homemade bread when I was little, and I treasure the bowl I still have that she used. Memories of our boxer running and grabbing the just-baked bread off of my dad's lap make the thought of cooking together even sweeter. Food in our life can be food for our soul, as we are fed by the moments we get to spend together, with food as a tool to draw us nearer to one another. When life gets complicated, the simplicity of home-cooked meals brings our souls back home.

Moms, plan a pause in your schedule at some point each week and just create with your tribe. Even during mayhem, a delight to tummies can help to mend our souls. We have created space for you to journal your special moments, too, in these pages. And don't let a diet keep you from having fun! Creations don't have to be unhealthy. Feel free to trade some ingredients in our recipes to fit your dietary needs. My oldest daughter has Celiac Disease, and we are able to successfully swap the flour for a gluten-free variety.

The moms who contributed to this book shared favorite recipes that knit their hearts with their children. We hope they will become your favorites, too. And our hope is that you will invite Jesus into your kitchen with you. As you make these recipes your own, read the Scriptures we share, talk about the things of God, sing worship songs, talk about life together, and how faith meets life's hard places. The kitchen is neutral ground where fresh faith can be found.

"Oh, taste and see that the Lord is good! Blessed is the man who takes refuge in him" (Psalm 34:8).

Denise

Table of Contents

A C K N O W L E D G M E N T S

I'm pretty sure most things in this life are done best when done in community. Iron sharpens iron and the gift of sharing dreams and ideas together is a treasure. Such is the blessing that God has given us.

I thank God for the ideas He gives and the ability to carry them out. It is hard sometimes, y'all, but so worth it. All that we go through in this life and learn from those experiences is not meant to be wasted but shared with others to help them as they form their own communities for the glory of God. Fiercely love the people around you, friends. They are the ones you get to do life with. And without them, you would not accomplish much of what you set your hand to.

Thank you, my darling husband, for serving with me in worship and speaking as we travel to share the hope that Christ offers. Thank you for being patient as I rose early or stayed up late with "one more idea."

Thank you, Seeing Deep team, for your hard work and love of God! You are a joy to work with!

Seeing Deep Team Contributors to this book and their role on the team:

Denise Pass	Founder/Director/Author	www.seeingdeep.com
Jennifer Elwood	Editor/Podcast Team Mgr.	www.jenniferelwood.com
Robin Gerblick	Social Media Engagement	www.exodusfitnessretreats.com
Tabatha Haines	Graphic Design	www.flawsoffriendship.com
Lisa Maples	Bible Tribe Podcast editor	www.lisamaples.life
Anne McCabe	Admin.	www.healthyabundant.life
Danielle Poorman	SD Podcast Devo Writer	www.daniellehope.com
Tonna Logan	Admin.	www.thebridgeoffaith.com

Spring Recipes

"Then I will send rain on your land in its season, both autumn and spring rains, so that you may gather in your grain, new wine and olive oil."
(Deuteronomy 11:14, ESV)

Oh, the delight of the blossoms that spring season brings! And there is so much fun to be had in the kitchen. The message of spring is new life. All things are new. Maybe try a new recipe or go outside for a picnic. Don't miss the opportunities that mealtime can bring. New conversations. New ways to share God's provision together. Join our team as we celebrate this season with recipes that turned our hearts toward God and toward one another.

Challah

BY JENNIFER ELWOOD

The Story behind the recipe:

As a family, we enjoy celebrating Jewish holidays. Doing life with Jesus for us means understanding His culture and the rhythm of celebrations He experienced. The type of bread in this recipe, Challah, is traditionally made by Jewish families for the evening meal of Shabbat (or Sabbath). Every Friday at sundown, candles are lit, and no work is performed for the next 24 hours. Families spend time reading Scripture and resting together, just as Jesus did with his family 2,000 years ago. We all need reminders to take rest. Perhaps the work of our hands making this wonderful bread will prepare us to enjoy a meal and unwind together.

Create some space for you and your family to pause and enjoy this recipe, reflecting on the multitudes of God's people who did the same as they reflected on God's goodness.

"SO THEN, THERE REMAINS A SABBATH REST FOR THE PEOLE OF GOD, FOR WHOEVER HAS ENTERED GOD'S REST HAS ALSO RESTED FROM HIS WORKS AS GOD DID FROM HIS."
—HEBREWS 4:9-10 (ESV)

Challah

"Come to me, all you who are weary and burdened, and I will give you rest" (Matthew 11:28, ESV).

INGREDIENTS

1 1/8 cup warm water
1 Tbs. dry yeast
1 tsp. sugar
2 eggs, plus an extra, beaten, to glaze bread
before baking
4 1/2 cups flour
1/2 Tbs. salt
1/2 cup sugar
1/4 cup vegetable oil
Optional sesame or poppy seeds

*Makes 2 loaves

DIRECTIONS

- Stir water, yeast and 1 tsp. sugar in small bowl.
- Whisk eggs, oil, sugar, and salt. Add liquified yeast. Add the flour until well incorporated.
- Knead on a floured surface for 15 minutes.
- Pour a little oil in a bowl to coat the bread and cover with a towel. Put in warm place for an hour until dough doubles in size.
- Punch down dough and knead again for a few minutes. Divide the dough in two.
- Place parchment paper on 2 baking sheets. Divide dough into three and gently roll into three strands, braid, and pinch ends together.
- Let dough rise an hour. Pre-heat oven to 350°.
- Brush dough with a beaten egg. Sprinkle with sesame or poppy seeds to add a little crunch.
- Bake 25-30 minutes until the top is golden.
- Shalom and enjoy!

YOUR MEMORIES

Easter Morning Monkey Bread

Special thanks to Dot Maples for making this recipe & Lisa Maples for the photo!

BY LISA MAPLES

The Story behind the recipe:

Since my children were small, my in-laws and parents have come to our home to spend the night before Easter. In the morning, we'd make Monkey Bread and place it in a cross-shaped pan. Something about the cross laying on our kitchen counter always reminded us that Jesus died for our sins then rose again on Easter morning!

Jesus referred to himself as the Bread of Life. Bread is satisfying, but we will not be fully satisfied unless we know Jesus. He satisfies our souls like no food or anything in this world can do. Just like bread or food are essential for our physical lives, so Jesus is essential for our spiritual lives. When we experience the sweet peace and joy that comes from knowing Him, we are filled with His presence and hope.

"JESUS SAID TO THEM, 'I AM THE BREAD OF LIFE. WHOEVER COMES TO ME SHALL NOT HUNGER, AND WHOEVER BELIEVES IN ME SHALL NEVER THIRST.'"
-JOHN 6:35 (ESV)

Easter Morning Monkey Bread

"But the angel said to the women, 'Do not be afraid; for I know that you are looking for Jesus who has been crucified. He is not here, for He has risen, just as He said [He would]. Come! See the place where He was lying'" (Matthew 28:5-6, AMP).

INGREDIENTS

1 cup sugar
1 1/4 tsp. cinnamon
3 cans butter-flavored canned biscuits
1 stick melted butter

Cross-shaped or Bundt pan

DIRECTIONS

- Preheat the oven to 350°.
- Combine sugar and cinnamon in a bowl.
- Open the three cans of butter-flavored biscuits and cut into bite-sized pieces.
- Toss biscuit pieces in cinnamon/sugar mixture.
- Place biscuit pieces in a greased, cross-shaped or Bundt pan.
- Combine leftover cinnamon and sugar with melted butter and sprinkle over the biscuits.
- Bake at 350° for 40 minutes.
- Remove from oven and turn over on a plate.
- Enjoy, because He is Risen! Hallelujah!

YOUR MEMORIES

_____

_____

_____

_____

Feed Your Friendships Sourdough Starter

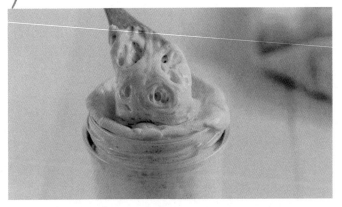

BY ANNE MCCABE

The Story behind the recipe:

My mother created this wonderful, rich sourdough recipe many times over the years and friends raved about how delicious it was. Doing life with Jesus is sharing love with friends and family from the kitchen. Home-baked goods can bring healing when they are shared with others in their time of need. The kitchen becomes a mission as we lovingly create and share. Also—the health benefits! Sourdough bread has superior health benefits when compared to other types of bread. It is great for the digestive system and resists spoiling.

This portion of the recipe is just the beginning. We always had sourdough starter handy growing up for a reason. Sharing this bread with family and friends was a fun way to create together and it multiplied our blessings over the years. I hope this recipe will bless you as much as it will feed your friendships for years to come.

"HE WHO SUPPLIES SEED TO THE SOWER AND BREAD FOR FOOD WILL SUPPLY AND MULTIPLY YOUR SEED FOR SOWING AND INCREASE THE HARVEST OF YOUR RIGHTEOUSNESS."
-2 CORINTHIANS 9:10 (ESV)

Feed My Friendships Sourdough Starter

"Jesus said to them, 'I am the bread of life; whoever comes to me shall not hunger, and whoever believes in me shall never thirst'" (John 6:35, ESV).

INGREDIENTS

Quick Starter Ingredients:
1 pkg. Dry yeast
1/2 cup lukewarm water
2 Tbs. sugar
2 cups warm water
2 1/2 Tbs. all-purpose flour

Sourdough Bread Feed:
3/4 cup sugar
1 cup warm water
3 Tbs. instant potatoes

DIRECTIONS

- Put together quick starter ingredients in refrigerator for 3 to 5 days.
- Combine sourdough bread feed ingredients and mix well. Take starter out of refrigerator and mix with sourdough bread feed.
- Let starter stand out of refrigerator all day (8-12 hours) or until very bubbly.
- Remove 1 cup to make bread and return remaining to refrigerator.
- Keep in refrigerator for 3 to 5 days then feed again.
- If not making bread after feeding starter, throw away 1 cup. Mixture may be fed 2 to 3 times before using to make bread.

YOUR MEMORIES

7

Feed My Friendships Sourdough Bread

BY ANNE MCCABE

The Story behind the recipe:

This recipe is a good example of perseverance in our faith. The beauty of the finished product is all in how we handle the starter. As with us, how we start in the faith matters, but will we finish well? If you have made the starter, your hard work and patience has paid off and it's time to make the bread! My mom made sourdough bread in small loaf pans throughout the year and made extras at Christmas time. She also generously shared the sourdough starter with others who wanted their kitchen full of the aroma that accompanies baking bread.

As a child, I have vivid memories of eating this bread fresh from the toaster with melted butter on it. It was so delicious! And this recipe has become precious to me and such a reminder of my mom every time I make it. There's no better time than right now to fill your kitchen with the aroma of bread and blessing as you prepare to surprise your family and friends with this delightful treat.

"A FRIEND LOVES AT ALL TIMES. A BROTHER IS BORN TO SHARE TROUBLES."
–PROVERBS 17:17 (NLT)

Feed My Friendships Sourdough Bread

"But he answered, 'It is written, Man shall not live by bread alone,
but by every word that comes from the mouth of God'" (Matthew 4:4, ESV).

INGREDIENTS

1/3 cup sugar
1/2 cup corn oil
1 Tbs. salt
1 cup sourdough starter (from previous recipe)
1 1/2 cups warm water
6 cups white bread flour

*Makes 3 loaves

DIRECTIONS

- Blend sugar, oil, salt, sourdough starter, water, and flour. This makes a stiff batter.
- Grease another bowl. Add dough and turn it over so it is greased on all sides.
- Lightly cover with foil and let stand overnight (do not refrigerate).
- Next morning punch down the dough. Knead a little.
- Divide into three and knead each part a few times on a floured board.
- Place into greased loaf pans and brush with oil.
- Cover with tea towel. Let rise until doubled, 4-5 hours or longer since dough rises slowly.
- Uncover and bake at 375° for 30-35 minutes or until an inserted toothpick comes out clean.
- Remove and brush with butter. Cool on rack.

YOUR MEMORIES

Hot Ham and Swiss Rolls

BY ANNE MCCABE

The Story behind the recipe:

Celebrations are a reminder that we have much to be thankful for. Food is an important part of the occasion that reminds us of the bounty God provides. This recipe was a favorite served at celebrations like bridal and baby showers. Delighting the soul and tummy, I noticed that people felt loved with the special foods that became our favorites.

I assisted my mom in making these rolls and my daughters carry on the tradition. This recipe is so delicious in its combination of flavors that people ask me for the recipe at every event I take them to! The hearty ham and buttery flavor make these rolls delightful. The Lord delights in our celebrations as we honor each other and bind our hearts in unity. Perhaps we can bring the atmosphere of celebration into our daily lives in some small ways. We don't have to wait for a special event to make a favorite dish.

"ALSO THAT EVERYONE SHOULD EAT AND DRINK AND TAKE PLEASURE IN AL HIS TOIL—
THIS IS GOD'S GIFT TO MAN."
—ECCLESIASTES 3:13 (ESV)

Hot Ham and Swiss Rolls

"Praise the LORD. How good it is to sing praises to our God,
how pleasant and fitting to praise him" (Psalm 147:1, NIV)!

INGREDIENTS

1 cup butter, softened
1 Tbs. poppyseeds
1 onion, finely chopped
3 Tbs. mustard
1 Tbs. Worcestershire sauce
2 pkg. dinner rolls
1-pound sliced ham
10 oz. Swiss Cheese slices

Optional: top with extra sprinkle of poppyseeds,
sesame seeds, or finely chopped parsley

DIRECTIONS

- Blend softened butter, poppy seed, onion, mustard, and Worcestershire sauce.
- Split both trays of rolls in half without separating into individual rolls.
- Spread butter mixture inside roll and reserve a little to brush on top. Add optional sprinkle of topping if desired.
- Cut rolls apart on dividing lines.
- Fill each roll with ham and swiss.
- Replace in original tray and cover with foil.
- Bake at 400° for 10 minutes.
- Remove foil and cook an additional 5 minutes until golden brown.
- Serve immediately and enjoy!

YOUR MEMORIES

Resurrection Rolls

Special thanks to Karen Hemming for making this recipe & Amber Trementozzi for the photo!

BY DENISE PASS

The Story behind the recipe:

Part of creating an atmosphere of awe and wonder on Easter morning was finding new ways to represent what Christ did on our behalf. The "oohs" and "ahs" from my children when these rolls were finished baking were soul satisfying, but so was the taste of these delicious rolls.

Doing life with Jesus starts in our homes and affects all we do. The kitchen is an important space that can be used to provide hospitality, nurturing, care—and fun! The comfort we find as we fellowship together in the kitchen and around the table is part of what knits our hearts together, especially during holidays. These Resurrection Rolls vividly convey the truth that our Savior is risen! The marshmallow is gone! And as we baked and ate these yummy rolls, we read Scriptures and reflected on the empty tomb a couple thousand years ago.

"AND HE SAID TO THEM, 'DO NOT BE ALARMED. YOU SEEK JESUS OF NAZARETH, WHO WAS CRUCIFIED. HE
HAS RISEN; HE IS NOT HERE. SEE THE PLACE WHERE THEY LAID HIM.'"
—MARK 16:6 (ESV)

Resurrection Rolls

"Blessed be the God and Father of our Lord Jesus Christ! According to his great mercy, he has caused us to be born again to a living hope through the resurrection of Jesus Christ from the dead" (1 Peter 1:3, ESV).

INGREDIENTS

16 large marshmallows
1/2 cup butter, melted
1/4 cup sugar
2 Tbs. cinnamon
2 (8-oz.) cans crescent roll dough*

*Can also substitute gluten-free dough

DIRECTIONS

- Combine sugar and cinnamon in a small bowl.
- Unroll crescent roll dough and separate each roll along perforations.
- Roll marshmallows in melted butter, then coat in cinnamon-sugar mixture. Place one coated marshmallow in the middle of the dough and roll the marshmallow until covered by the dough. Pinch seams to seal each roll.
- Place rolls on a greased pan and bake at 350° for about 12 minutes.
- Immediately after removing rolls from the oven, brush with remaining melted butter and then sprinkle with remaining cinnamon-sugar mixture. Serve warm.

YOUR MEMORIES

Savory Broccoli Cornbread

BY ANNE MCCABE

The Story behind the recipe:

Every mom knows the protocol when something green and healthy hits the table. Avoid or hide the food to make it look like you ate it. But have no fear! This recipe is a fun, delicious way to get more healthy vegetables in our children and is easy to make. The combination of sweet cornbread and savory broccoli together is delicious.

Part of our nurturing is nutrition. As we know from the Bible, Daniel and his friends had good results from eating vegetables and avoiding all the rich foods from the king's table. Teaching our children to be disciplined in their nutrition is a blessing to them physically and spiritually. It also helps them to not be picky when they are faced with food that is not their favorite. Let's be grateful for all the wonderful food the Lord has made, especially the veggies!

"AT THE END OF TEN DAYS IT WAS SEEN THAT THEY WERE BETTER IN APPEARANCE AND FATTER IN FLESH THAN ALL THE YOUTHS WHO ATE THE KING'S FOOD. SO THE STEWARD TOOK AWAY THEIR FOOD AND THE WINE THEY WERE TO DRINK, AND GAVE THEM VEGETABLES."
—DANIEL 1:15-16 (ESV)

Savory Broccoli Cornbread

"So, whether you eat or drink, or whatever you do, do all to the glory of God" (1 Corinthians 10:31, ESV).

INGREDIENTS

1—10 oz. pkg. frozen, chopped broccoli (room temperature)
1 box Jiffy corn muffin mix*
4 eggs
1 stick butter
6 oz. cottage cheese
1 large onion, chopped
1/2 tsp. salt

*Can also substitute a healthier cornbread recipe

DIRECTIONS

- Mix all ingredients together except butter.
- Melt the butter.
- Mix in with the rest of ingredients and pour into pan.
- Bake at 350° for 30 minutes or until golden brown.
- Savor the amazing flavors and enjoy!

YOUR MEMORIES

_____

_____

_____

_____

Soft French Bread

BY DENISE PASS

The Story behind the recipe:

This recipe is worn out in my cookbook. Residual stains from splatters of ingredients over the years make me smile. My family loved it when I would make this recipe. The joy on their faces and the fast-disappearing bread were indicators. And for you budget conscious moms— this recipe is easy and cheap to make! Having home-baked bread at the dinner table communicated that I took extra time to make something for them. It also had a way of beckoning the family together and uniting us around the table when lives began to get too busy.

Bread is an important food in the Bible, mentioned over 400 times. God provided Manna from Heaven to the Israelites in the desert. Similarly, Jesus shared bread with thousands as He prayed, and the bread was multiplied. Sharing bread together is a reminder that God first shared it with us.

"BUT HE ANSWERED, 'IT IS WRITTEN, MAN SHALL NOT LIVE BY BREAD ALONE,
BUT BY EVERY WORD THAT COMES FROM THE MOUTH OF GOD.'"
–MATTHEW 4:4 (ESV)

Soft French Bread

"Now as they were eating, Jesus took bread, and after blessing it broke it and gave it to the disciples, and said, 'Take, eat; this is my body'" (Matthew 26:26, ESV).

INGREDIENTS

2 pkg. dry yeast
1/2 cup warm water
1/2 tsp. sugar
2 Tbs. sugar
2 Tbs. coconut oil or Crisco
2 tsp. salt
2 cups boiling water
7 1/2 - 8 cups of flour
1 egg, beaten
2 Tbs. milk
Poppy or sesame seeds, optional

DIRECTIONS

- Dissolve the first three ingredients, set aside.
- Combine the sugar, oil, salt and boiling H_2O.
- Cool the mixture to lukewarm and add yeast mixture.
- Stir in flour.
- Knead for 10 minutes or until smooth.
- Place in greased bowl, turning once. Let rise until doubled.
- Punch down dough and rest for 15 minutes.
- Divide dough in half, roll each out on floured surface into a rectangle. Roll up into loaves.
- Place loaves on greased cookie sheets and slash 4-5 times across the top.
- Rise until double, mix egg and milk then brush on top. Sprinkle on optional seeds, if desired.
- Bake at 400° for 20 minutes.

YOUR MEMORIES

Summer Recipes

**"As soon as they come out in leaf, you see for yourselves
and know that the summer is already near."
(Luke 21:30, ESV)**

As the kids were growing up, the yearning for summer grew, too. We could not wait for the hot summer days and the melting popsicles. Fun field trips to the chocolate or pretzel factory followed up by picnics featuring our own homespun creations made summer even more memorable!

Don't miss the opportunity that summer brings! Maybe hot kitchens are not too inviting but baking early in the morning can help to solve that dilemma! Involving little hands that perhaps rose earlier than you were ready for also helps to turn mundane moments into treasured memories. Get out with your tribe and bring some of these yummy culinary creations with you as you explore God's beautiful creation. Talk about the things of God and His precious word while you enjoy His provision!

Best Ever Butter Cookies

BY ROBIN GERBLICK

The Story behind the recipe:

When I was a child, my mom made these cookies and we made them disappear. I mean… really disappear! Once she made the dough, she rolled it into logs and placed them in the freezer for future use. The problem was we knew where the dough was and, you know, everyone loves raw cookie dough, right? My poor mom was ready to bake, and it was completely gone. Time to make a new batch and start the whole process all over again.

As sweet as these delectable cookies are, it was my mom's willingness to keep making them that demonstrated something to me more than the recipe itself. How we serve our families in our baking and making of food lasts longer than the food itself. I thank God for my mom's sense of humor and her persistence to keep making those cookies. That tradition continues today with our kids, grandkids, and extended family. No one can escape the cookie dough monster!

"INDEED, HOW CAN PEOPLE AVOID WHAT THEY DON'T KNOW IS GOING TO HAPPEN?"
—ECCLESIASTES 8:7 (NLT)

Best Ever Butter Cookies

"We were filled with laughter, and we sang for joy. And the other nations said, 'What amazing things the LORD has done for them'" (Psalm 126:2, NLT).

INGREDIENTS

2 1/2 cups sifted cake flour
1 cup butter
1 cup sugar
1 tsp vanilla
2 egg yolks
1 egg white
Optional toppings of choice: Our favorites include chocolate sprinkles or chopped nuts with cinnamon sugar.

DIRECTIONS

- Sift flour and set aside.
- Cream butter and sugar.
- Add vanilla, egg yolks and egg white.
- Beat well, then add flour.
- Chill dough, shape the dough into logs 1 1/2-inches diameter by 10-inches long.
- Wrap logs in foil and freeze until ready to use.
- When ready to bake, preheat oven to 350°.
- Slice frozen log into 1/4-inch slices, dip the top side of cookie in egg white then in topping of your choice.
- Bake at 350° for 15 minutes.
- Keep safe from the cookie monster and enjoy!

YOUR MEMORIES

_____

_____

_____

_____

Elizabeth's Blueberry Pie

BY TABATHA HAINES

The Story behind the recipe:

Cooking creates wonderful memories for the heart and soul. The things we taste, and smell, can take us back to happy times in the kitchen. I've learned moments become memories, and memories can eventually be the only things we have left with those we love most. My first recipe was handed down to me by a friend who moved away soon after. When we share handwritten recipes with our loved ones, they keep a piece of us with them forever.

I will always cherish this wonderful recipe and be reminded of the time I spent with my beloved friend. Sharing recipes is a small way we can share ourselves with those we love, so the next time you make a meal that someone enjoys, handwrite the recipe for them. Give it to them as a gift of making memories from one heart and kitchen to another.

"A GOOD MAN LEAVES AN INHERITANCE TO HIS CHILDREN'S CHILDREN."
–PROVERBS 13:32a (NKJV)

Elizabeth's Blueberry Pie

"You will enjoy the fruit of your labor. How joyful and prosperous you will be" (Psalm 128:2, NLT)!

INGREDIENTS

1 Pie Shell (gluten-free, if desired).

Filling:
1 cup or 3/4 can blueberry filling
Big handful of fresh or frozen blueberries
1/2 cup sugar
1/4 cup lemon juice

Topping:
1/2 cup butter
1/2 cup brown sugar
1/2 cup crushed cereal (Chex or other)

DIRECTIONS

- Preheat the oven to 350°.
- Heat pie shell for 5 minutes or so before filling (for a flakier crust).
- Mix blueberries and filling with sugar and lemon juice.
- Fill the pie shell.
- Soften butter and add to cereal mix, spread over the pie.
- Bake 30 minutes on 350°.
- Enjoy the sweet taste of summer with your family!

YOUR MEMORIES

_____

_____

_____

_____

Eat Play Dough

BY DENISE PASS

The Story behind the recipe:

As moms, we can forget to have fun. Misbehavior, dirty diapers, and lack of sleep can contribute to life feeling pretty mundane. But moms, we have a holy calling. God has entrusted us with His kids—to raise them to know and love Him. This holy calling should also be fun! When we get down on our kid's level, our children feel like we can relate to them. This recipe was a favorite in my house, my now adult kids remember this well. While we molded, played, and took bites we would giggle and talk about the things of God and mold objects with the dough that sparked faith and conversations that laid a foundation for years to come.

Playing with our kids creates more than just joy and wonder. Trust is built there, too.

"IMPRESS THEM ON YOUR CHILDREN. TALK ABOUT THEM WHEN YOU SIT AT HOME AND WHEN YOU WALK ALONG THE ROAD. WHEN YOU LIE DOWN AND WHEN YOU GET UP. IMPRESS THEM ON YOUR CHILDREN. TALK ABOUT THEM WHEN YOU SIT AT HOME AND WHEN YOU WALK ALONG THE ROAD, WHEN YOU LIE DOWN AND WHEN YOU GET UP."
—DEUTERONOMY 6:6-7 (NIV)

Eat Play Dough

"And the streets of the city shall be full of boys and girls playing in its streets" (Zechariah 8:5, ESV).

INGREDIENTS

1/3 cup margarine
1/2 tsp. salt
1/3 cup light corn syrup
1 tsp. vanilla
1-pound Confectioners' sugar
Food coloring if desired

DIRECTIONS

- Mix the first four ingredients with an electric mixer.
- When combined, add the powdered sugar and continue to mix well.
- Knead the dough until smooth.
- Divide into desired portions and color each with natural food colors, if desired.
- Store in containers or Ziploc bags.
- Refrigerate to prevent spoiling.

YOUR MEMORIES

Edible Sandcastle Cake

Special thanks to Dot Maples for making this recipe & for Lisa Maples for the photo!

BY LISA MAPLES

The Story behind the recipe:

Vacation is an opportunity to create together in the kitchen! When my family visits the beach, we pack our castle-shaped pan and ingredients. My children and I love creating a sandcastle cake each summer. When we need a break from the rain or sun, we bake! This has become a part of our family heritage. Decorating is my children's favorite part. Blue frosting around and up to the castle base represents the ocean. Then we add various candies we've accumulated, shake some fish-shaped sprinkles on, and add a few small umbrellas. When we work together on a project, it unites our hearts and each one takes delight in their part, as well as the completed project. The pictures through the years are priceless, too! Having fun traditions incorporated into our time together helps to form beautiful memories.

"MIGHTIER THAN THE THUNDERS OF MANY WATERS, MIGHTIER THAN THE WAVES OF THE SEA, THE LORD ON HIGH IS MIGHTY!"
—PSALM 93:4 (RSV)

Edible Sandcastle Cake

"A joyful heart is good medicine, but a crushed spirit dries up the bones" (Proverbs 17:22, ESV).

INGREDIENTS

1 castle-shaped Bundt style pan
1 box of yellow cake mix, eggs and oil as stated on the box
Non-stick cooking spray
Flour for dusting the pan
1 container white frosting
Blue food coloring
Other decorating ideas:
Fish-shaped sprinkles, Swedish fish candy, aquatic animal-shaped gummies, paper umbrellas

DIRECTIONS

- Spray pan, place dusting of flour in the pan then pour out remaining.
- Preheat oven based on the cake box directions.
- Mix cake using box directions and pour into a greased pan. Bake for recommended Bundt pan time.
- Allow cake to cool.
- Turn cake over on decorative tray.
- Use the dyed frosting to create waves.
- Use selected candies to decorate.
- Don't forget to take a picture and enjoy!

YOUR MEMORIES

Betty's Dirt Cups

BY DENISE PASS

The Story behind the recipe:

My husband has fond memories of his momma's cooking over the years. She has handed down cookbooks that are a legacy for those who come behind her. Grandma Betty, as all her grandchildren knew her by, hosted many gatherings. While we all would joke that it was "all about the food," we all knew within our hearts that it was all about the love. The song we would sing while we patiently waited, the extra care in food preparation and the faith that we shared made times together a treasure. And now that Betty is in Heaven dancing with Jesus, her memory is with us as we cook recipes and hold cookbooks that her hands also held. Sometimes our cooking does not have to be extravagant to make a big impact. This fun recipe is perfect for a quick treat with kids or grandkids. Sometimes easy creations in the kitchen help us to bring special moments into our days without a lot of hoopla. And we don't always have to have a reason to do something special.

"THE MEMORY OF THE RIGHTEOUS IS A BLESSING . . ."
–PROVERBS 10:7 (ESV)

Betty's Dirt Cups

"How sweet are your words to my taste, sweeter than honey to my mouth" (Psalm 119:103, ESV)!

INGREDIENTS

2 cups cold milk
1 pkg. 4 serving Jell-o Chocolate pudding mix
1 tub 8 oz. Cool Whip, thawed (sugar-free if desired)
1—16 oz. pkg Oreos, crushed (gluten-free if desired)
10—7 oz. plastic cups
Suggested decorations:
Gummy worms and frogs, candy flowers, chopped peanuts

DIRECTIONS

- Pour milk into a large bowl.
- Add pudding mix
- Beat with whisk until well blended, 1-2 minutes.
- Let stand for 5 minutes.
- Stir in whipped topping and half of crushed cookies.
- Place 1 Tbs. crushed cookies into cups.
- Fill cups 3/4 full of pudding mixture.
- Top with remaining crushed cookies.
- Refrigerate 1 hour.
- Decorate with your choice of goodies.

YOUR MEMORIES

_____

_____

_____

_____

29

Chocolate Chip Pie

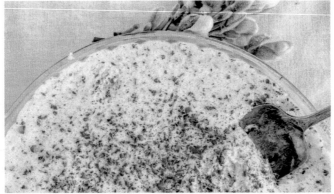

Special thanks to Jennifer Elwood for making this recipe & for taking the photo!

BY JENNIFER ELWOOD

The Story behind the recipe:

This delicious recipe passed through my family from my great-grandma Yantzer to my grandma Hildagarde Frank. When I consider the words in our verse, it reminds me of how much the women in my family, reaching back at least three generations, love Jesus. Our faith is woven into all we make and do, and recipes are a beautiful way of passing our faith down, too.

This pie typically marks celebration and every person in our family loves it. The memory of sweet marshmallow and bitter chocolate lingers in our thoughts from the moment we melt the marshmallows until it arrives at the table. As you create this delicious pie, consider people from your past and how they influenced the faith you have today. Then send the Lord a thank you prayer for placing these people in your lives!

"I AM REMINDED OF YOUR SINCERE FAITH, A FAITH THAT DWELT FIRST IN YOUR GRANDMOTHER LOUIS AND YOUR MOTHER EUNICE AND NOW, I AM SURE, DWELLS IN YOU AS WELL."
-2 TIMOTHY 1:5 (ESV)

Chocolate Chip Pie

"So then, brothers and sisters, stand firm and hold [tightly] to the traditions which you were taught, whether by word of mouth or by letter from us" (2 Thessalonians 2:15, AMP).

INGREDIENTS

Filling:
30 marshmallows
1/2 cup milk
2 squares unsweetened chocolate, grated
1/2 pint whipping cream, beaten

Graham Cracker Crust:
12 graham crackers, crushed
1/2 cup melted butter

Alternatively, purchase a crust from the store

DIRECTIONS

- Crush the graham crackers and fully incorporate with melted butter.
- Press the mixture into a thin layer on the base of a pie plate and up the sides.
- Melt marshmallows in a double boiler or on low with 1/2 cup milk.
- Fold marshmallows gently into the whipped cream and add the grated chocolate.
- Pour into the graham cracker shell and chill for a few hours to set.
- Celebrate the goodness of the Lord to your family as you dig in!

YOUR MEMORIES

31

Orange You Sweet Teacake

Special thanks to Shannon Looby for making this recipe & Amber Trementozzi for the photo!

BY ANNE MCCABE

The Story behind the recipe:

This was a beloved recipe in my mom's collection. Creating this delicious dessert is made more special by the hands that work together to make it. Enjoyable to make together with loved ones, hand-braiding the dough is a fun, tactile way of involving children. This recipe is like a project, which provides opportunities for conversation and creating together.

This teacake requires some fruit of the spirit: patience. But its delicate sweetness is worth the effort! It has active steps including kneading, braiding, and waiting. . . which make the end result satisfying! Perseverance and hard work, baking together with Jesus, creates memories and yields good fruit.

"DO YOU SEE A MAN SKILLFUL IN HIS WORK? HE WILL STAND BEFORE KINGS;
HE WILL NOT STAND BEFORE OBSCURE MEN."
—PROVERBS 22:29 (ESV)

Orange You Sweet Teacake

"Let us not become weary in doing good, for at the proper time we will reap a harvest if we do not give up" (Galatians 6:9, NIV).

INGREDIENTS

1 pkg. active dry yeast
1/4 cup warm water
1/2 cup warm milk (105-115° F)
1/2 cup fresh orange juice
1/2 cup granulated sugar
1/2 cup ricotta cheese
1 Tbs. grated orange zest
1/2 teaspoon salt
1 large egg, lightly beaten
3 1/2 - 4 cups all-purpose flour
Glaze: 1 large egg, lightly beaten
Icing: 1 cup confectioners' sugar and 2 Tbs. fresh orange juice, whisked together

DIRECTIONS

- Dissolve yeast in warm water, 5 to 10 minutes. Mix milk, orange juice, sugar, ricotta cheese, orange zest, salt, and egg into yeast mixture.
- Knead on lightly floured surface until smooth and elastic, 5 to 10 minutes.
- Place dough in a greased bowl, turning to coat. Cover and rise until doubled, about 1 1/2 hours.
- Punch down dough. Knead 1 to 2 minutes.
- Divide dough into 3 pieces. Roll each into 20-inch rope, braid, and coil in a greased, 10-inch springform pan. Tuck ends under. Cover, raise until almost doubled, 30 minutes.
- Preheat oven to 425°.
- Brush dough with egg glaze. Bake until golden brown, 25-30 minutes. Turn cake out and cool.
- Spread icing over warm cake, serve, and enjoy!

YOUR MEMORIES

Saintly Strawberry Pie

BY ANNE MCCABE

The Story behind the recipe:

Served at picnics and cookouts on hot summer days this pie is a welcome refreshment to all. It is perfect for patriotic celebrations in the US because the cool whip topping can be decorated with strawberries and blueberries for a red, white, and blue effect.

To make this pie more of a project with children, take them out strawberry picking first. Doing life with Jesus means creating opportunities for our children to work beside us. Working together side-by-side gives our children a good work ethic and makes the process so satisfying. The memories shared in creating the pie are tied to the events and people we share them with. And our children's confidence is boosted when their labor is acknowledged. The secret is that this recipe is so easy to make and so yummy!

"BLESSED IS THE NATION WHOSE GOD IS THE LORD,
THE PEOPLE HE CHOSE FOR HIS INHERITANCE."
-PSALM 33:12 (NIV)

Saintly Strawberry Pie

"But the Holy Spirit produces this kind of fruit in our lives: love, joy, peace, patience, kindness, goodness, faithfulness, gentleness, and self-control. There is no law against these things" (Galatians 5:22-23, NLT)!

INGREDIENTS

Two baked pie shells

Filling:
1/2 cup sugar
1/4 cup cornstarch, pressed firmly into the cup
1/4 cup cold water
2 1/2 cups boiling water
1 pkg. strawberry gelatin
5 cups strawberries

Topping:
Cool Whip, optional extra fruit

DIRECTIONS

- Mix cornstarch with 1/4 cup cold water.
- Add sugar and cornstarch mixture to boiling water. Continue boiling and stirring until the liquid is clear.
- Remove from heat and stir in strawberry gelatin.
- Allow to cool a few minutes and add strawberries.
- Pour into two baked pie shells and refrigerate.
- Cover with Cool Whip and decorative fruit, if desired, before serving.
- Enjoy the smiles and conversations sparked from creating together!

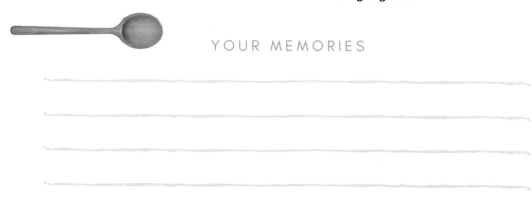

YOUR MEMORIES

Fall Recipes

"While the earth remains, seedtime and harvest, cold and heat, summer and winter, day and night, shall not cease." (Genesis 8:22, ESV)

There is something about the crisp days of autumn that invite us to reflect. Lit candles and crackling fireplaces remind us of days gone by and the sweet smell of cinnamon drifting through the house sets an atmosphere of home. The baked goods in the oven complete the picture of fall as we look toward the winter ahead.

In each season, we can share in the love of God in our homes with our families as we infuse our faith in all we do. Baking for church events, family get-togethers, or for friends in need, our kitchens become a mission.

Chicken Pot Pie

BY DANIELLE POORMAN

The Story behind the recipe:

Savory dishes have a way of making us feel safe and taken care of. And when they are yummy, they hold a place in our heart, too. Teaching our children how to cook and create for their future families is part of their discipleship.

Chicken Pot Pie was one of my absolute favorite dishes as a child. Growing up in Northern Maine, I craved something warm and cozy for dinner. Over the years, I experimented with different twists on this cherished, classic dish. Then, one day, a friend served us chicken pot pie baked in a springform pan. The deep flavors popped, the crust was flaky, and my kiddos ate it up! Spread and nestled inside a pie plate or even in a small frying pan for a fun alternate way of presentation, this dish is the essence of fall. But we confess to enjoying it all year long and it is my son's favorite dinner request.

"COME TO ME ALL WHO LABOR AND ARE HEAVY LADEN, AND I WILL GIVE YOU REST."
—MATTHEW 11:28 (ESV)

Chicken Pot Pie

"Oh give thanks to the Lord, for he is good, for his steadfast love endures forever" (Psalm 107:1, ESV)!

INGREDIENTS

2 9-inch refrigerated pie crusts
3 carrots, peeled and diced
2 russet potatoes, peeled and diced
1 onion, peeled and diced
3 cloves garlic, peeled and diced
1 sprig fresh rosemary
2 sprigs fresh thyme
2 cooked, shredded boneless/skinless chicken breasts (or precooked rotisserie chicken)
2 Tbs. butter
1/4 cup flour
1/2 - 1 cup chicken stock
2 Tbs. olive oil
salt and pepper to taste
cooking spray

DIRECTIONS

- Preheat oven to 375°.
- Heat Dutch oven or large skillet over medium heat, melt butter and olive oil.
- Sauté onions, carrots, and potatoes for 7-8 minutes until tender. Add garlic and herbs, cook 3 minutes. Mixture should be *almost* fork tender.
- Add shredded chicken and splash of chicken stock, stir.
- Sprinkle in flour. Stir and cook for 1 minute. Add rest of stock and cook 1 minute. Mixture should thicken. Remove from heat and set aside.
- Line a 9-inch pie plate with one crust and poke a few holes. Spoon in chicken mixture and spread evenly. Cover with other crust. Fold the top crust under the bottom and flute edges.
- Bake 40-45 minutes until golden brown. Enjoy!

YOUR MEMORIES

Chocolate Drop Oatmeal Cookies

BY DENISE PASS

The Story behind the recipe:

These cookies have been a closely guarded secret for many years. So shhhh! Keep this one safe. My husband's momma always had these cookies on hand and when I finally got my hands on this recipe, I created it for my tribe on Friday nights or on vacations. Baking cookies spoke love to my children. It meant I took extra time out of my schedule and it also meant games, or a movie night were a likely accompaniment to this delicious treat.

When fellowship surrounds our culinary creations, the enjoyment is all the sweeter. Now my children bake their own cookies to bring home and the tradition lives on. As you prepare these cookies, consider who God might have you share them with. Our cooking can be a mission when we share with those who could use some encouragement. Just as cookies are pleasant to our tastebuds, they can sweeten someone's day!

"SO THEN, BROTHERS, STAND FIRM AND HOLD TO THE TRADITIONS THAT YOU WERE TAUGHT BY US, EITHER BY OUR SPOKEN WORD OR BY OUR LETTER."
-2 THESSALONIANS 2:15 (ESV)

Chocolate Drop Oatmeal Cookies

"And all the believers met together in one place and shared everything they had" (Acts 2:44, NLT).

INGREDIENTS

1 cup Crisco
1 cup brown sugar
1 cup granulated sugar
2 eggs
1 tsp. vanilla
2 cups plain flour (or gluten-free)
1/2 tsp. salt
1 tsp. baking soda
3 cups rolled oats
1—12 oz. pkg. chocolate drops
Alternate variation: Substitute 1 cup raisins and 1/2 cup chopped nuts for the chocolate chips or add them to the recipe.

DIRECTIONS

- Preheat oven to 325°.
- Cream together Crisco and sugars until light and fluffy.
- Add eggs one at a time and beat well.
- Add vanilla and blend.
- Sift together flour, salt and baking soda, add to creamed mixture.
- Stir in chocolate drops and oatmeal.
- Drop from a spoon on ungreased cookie sheet.
- Bake for about 10 minutes.
- Remove from pan and enjoy!

YOUR MEMORIES

41

Healthy & Creamy Chicken Jalapeno Popper Soup

BY DENISE PASS

The Story behind the recipe:

When we are in the throes of raising our children, we don't get the benefit of looking into the future to see how they will turn out. Mommas, when we are faithful to ground our children in the word of God and put Christ in the center of our lives, God's Word promises that we will bear fruit. With mostly adult children now, God has proven Himself to be faithful. Sometimes parenting is chaotic and messy. Don't let that deter you from the task that God has given us to do—raising kids for His glory, not ours. Wherever you are at in your parenting days, keep looking to Jesus. This recipe is precious to me because my oldest daughter and I are continuing on the foundation laid—time together in the kitchen with Jesus. She and her husband brought this delicious recipe to share together at our home. The joy in my daughter's eyes that now she was cooking and bringing the food to share was priceless! This recipe is adapted from a Trim Healthy Momma (THM) recipe. Enjoy!

"AND I AM CERTAIN THAT GOD, WHO BEGAN THE GOOD WORK WITHIN YOU, WILL CONTINUE HIS WORK UNTIL IT IS FINALLY FINISHED ON THE DAY WHEN CHRIST JESUS RETURNS."
—PHILIPPIANS 1:6 (NASB)

Healthy & Creamy Chicken Jalapeno Popper Soup

"All your children shall be taught by the LORD, and great shall be the peace of your children"
(Isaiah 54:13, ESV).

INGREDIENTS

2-pounds cooked and chopped chicken breast
6 jalapeño peppers (sliced/remove seeds)
1 onion
2 red bell peppers
2 garlic cloves
2 Tbsp. butter
32 oz. bag cauliflower
4 cups water
4 bouillon cubes
8 oz. low-fat cream cheese
1 cup black beans, drained
2 tomatoes, chopped
12 oz. salsa
4 tsp. chili powder
2 tsp. cumin
1 tsp. salt

DIRECTIONS

- Sauté chicken in a pan with cooking spray, cut into small pieces and set aside.
- Dice vegetables and sauté in butter with the garlic for 3-5 minutes.
- Remove veggies from pot and set aside.
- Cook cauliflower, water and chicken bouillon cubes in pot until tender.
- Blend cream cheese in blender.
- Add cauliflower to blender and blend until smooth.
- Combine all of the ingredients in the pot and simmer on medium-low heat until ready, 15-30 minutes.
- This soup will knock your socks off!
- Garnish with shredded cheese if desired.

YOUR MEMORIES

43

I Love Cheeseburgers Medley

Special thanks to Michelle Fowler for making this recipe & Amber Trementozzi for the photo!

BY ANNE MCCABE

The Story behind the recipe:

There is something satisfying about making a hearty meal for all to enjoy. Conversations flow and smiles abound when palates are pleased. Jesus showed us how to provide delicious food and to talk about the things of God. Mealtimes have a purpose. And when the food is delicious, we have a captive audience, providing an opportunity to talk about the things of life through the lens of faith.

The flavor of cheeseburger with a flaky, golden crust is absolutely delicious! It was in my mom's collection and made a comforting dinner. I remember standing by the stove, cooking ground beef on busy nights when mom needed my help to put a simple dinner together. It always made me feel good to help mom while creating something my whole family enjoyed.

"WHATEVER YOU DO, WORK HEARTILY, AS FOR THE LORD AND NOT FOR MEN, KNOWING THAT FROM THE LORD YOU WILL RECEIVE THE INHERITANCE AS YOUR REWARD. YOU ARE SERVING THE LORD CHRIST."
-COLOSSIANS 3:23-24 (ESV)

I Love Cheeseburger Medley

"Love one another with brotherly affection. Outdo one another in showing honor" (Romans 12:10, ESV).

INGREDIENTS

9-inch pie crust pastry
1-pound ground beef
1/4 cup green pepper, chopped
1/4 cup onion, chopped
4 oz. tomato sauce
1/2 cup dry breadcrumbs
1/2 tsp. Italian seasoning
1/4 tsp. pepper
1/4 tsp. salt
1 egg, beaten
1/4 cup milk
1 tsp. mustard
1 tsp. Worcestershire sauce
2 cups (8 oz.) shredded cheddar cheese

DIRECTIONS

- Preheat oven to 400°.
- Line 9-inch pie pan with pastry. Trim excess around edges, prick bottom and sides of pastry with fork. Bake 8 minutes.
- Cook ground beef, green pepper, salt, and onion in a large skillet until meat is browned, breaking apart to crumble, then drain.
- Combine tomato sauce, breadcrumbs, Italian seasoning, and pepper, stirring well.
- Spoon mixture into prepared crust.
- Combine egg, milk, mustard, Worcestershire sauce, and cheese, stir well, spoon evenly over top of the meat.
- Bake at 375° for 30 minutes.
- Enjoy!

YOUR MEMORIES

Mom's TV Snack Mix

BY ROBIN GERBLICK

The Story behind the recipe:

Working on projects together can be so satisfying. It reminds me of the body of Christ—each part of the body is equally as significant, yet unique in its role. Sounds deep for a party mix, but sometimes it takes the simple things to be able to convey the deeper things of Christ to our loved ones.

I remember making this with both my mom and dad. . . a family project with all the kids. But truth be told, it truly is my dad's secret recipe. I'm giving mom credit for the title of the recipe because she always added an extra ingredient. . . love! Her tender care to mix the ingredients over and over again added the special touch that kept us coming back for more. This recipe is now a family tradition passed down through the generations. My daughter makes it for her girls but, shhh, don't tell anyone . . . her version is better than my dad's!

"HONOR YOUR FATHER AND MOTHER. THEN YOU WILL LIVE A LONG,
FULL LIFE IN THE LAND THE LORD YOUR GOD IS GIVING YOU."
—EXODUS 20:12 (NLT)

Mom's TV Snack Mix

"Be completely humble and gentle; be patient, bearing with one another in love" (Ephesians 4:2, NIV).

INGREDIENTS

Snack Mixture:
4 cups each: Cheerios, Crispix, Wheat Chex, Rice Chex
4 cups salted mixed nuts
4 cups pretzels
2 Tbs. Worcestershire Sauce
2 Tbs. Tabasco Sauce
1/4-pound butter
1/4-pound bacon grease—our family's secret ingredient that makes this recipe delicious! But you can substitute 1/4-pound butter if desired.

Salt Mixture:
1 Tbs. celery salt
1 Tbs. Lawry's seasoning salt
1 1/2 Tbs. garlic powder

DIRECTIONS

- Melt together butter, bacon grease (if using), Worcestershire and Tabasco sauces.
- Place all dry ingredients in a large roasting pan and mix.
- Spoon melted sauce mixture over dry ingredients and mix thoroughly.
- Sprinkle salt mixture evenly over the coated ingredients, tossing several times.
- Bake in 250° oven for 2-2 1/2 hours, mixing every half hour (with love).
- Enjoy with family and friends for a movie night!

YOUR MEMORIES

Puffy Pancakes

BY DANIELLE POORMAN

The Story behind the recipe:

Part of the joy of cooking with our children is imparting our faith and cooking skills down to them. As they learn how to make different recipes, they are also learning the things of God—a double win! One of my fondest childhood memories is of weekend breakfasts as a little girl. Waking up to the smell of sizzling pancakes on the griddle was the best! My mom loved teaching me how to make this recipe that passed through generations. Now, I love teaching my children how to make them. Their eyes gleam when I ask, "who's going to flip this one?"

A family twist on a basic pancake recipe, this one is simple and extremely versatile for any seasonal mood. Add berries or seasonal fruit—this recipe is for all seasons. This was the first recipe I learned to make as a child, and I will always cherish that memory.

"SO, WHETHER YOU EAT OR DRINK, OR WHATEVER YOU DO, DO ALL TO THE GLORY OF GOD."
—1 CORINTHIANS 10:31 (ESV)

48

Puffy Pancakes

"For this very reason, make every effort to supplement your faith with virtue,
and virtue with knowledge" (2 Peter 1:5, ESV).

INGREDIENTS

2 eggs
Dash of vanilla
1 cup milk, or any milk alternative
4 Tbs. melted butter
2 cups all-purpose flour
1/4 cup white sugar
1 Tbs. baking powder
pinch of salt
1 tsp. ground cinnamon
Dash of allspice

*We love adding seasonal ingredients: dark-chocolate chips, berries, or bananas.
Yummy! Make it your own.

DIRECTIONS

- Heat griddle pan to medium heat.
- Mix eggs and milk together well.
- Add melted butter and mix briefly.
- Add flour, sugar, baking powder, salt, and cinnamon.
- Let batter sit and thicken for a few minutes. If it is too thick, splash in a little milk.
- Drop by 1/4 cups onto hot griddle. When you see bubbles after about 3 minutes, it's time to flip. Cook another 3 minutes.
- Transfer to a plate and keep going until the batter is gone.
- Serve with your favorite syrup and toppings.
- Enjoy!

YOUR MEMORIES

"Punkin Pie"

BY TONNA LOGAN

The Story behind the recipe:

Don't let the name fool you! This is an old-fashioned pumpkin pie with a whole lotta added love and bursting with flavor. When I held my middle granddaughter Henli for the first time, I called her pumpkin and the nickname stuck. When she started to speak, she referred to me as "punkin," which became my special "grandma" name. Since then, we've begun a tradition of baking pumpkin pies together with thoughts of this term of endearment. I hope this recipe, and special grandma name, will be passed down for years to come.

Christ's message speaks to generations. Just like we pass down names and recipes, we have an opportunity to pass down the heritage we have in Christ. When our faith is passed down daily, lives and generations are changed.

"AS A MOTHER COMFORTS HER CHILD, SO WILL I COMFORT YOU;
AND YOU WILL BE COMFORTED OVER JERUSALEM."
-ISAIAH 66:13 (NIV)

"Punkin Pie"

"For he satisfies the thirsty and fills the hungry with good things" (Psalm 107:9, NIV).

INGREDIENTS

1/2 tsp. pepper
1/2 tsp. nutmeg
1/2 tsp. ginger
1 tsp. cinnamon
1/2 tsp. salt
3/4 cup sugar
1 tsp. vanilla
1—14 oz. can sweetened condensed milk
2 large eggs
1—15 oz. can of pumpkin pie filling
1 frozen pie crust, defrosted

DIRECTIONS

- Preheat oven to 425°.
- Whisk 2 large eggs and can of milk.
- In another bowl, mix pumpkin pie filling, spices, salt and sugar.
- Gradually add the egg/milk mixture while whisking until smooth.
- Pour mixture into pie crust.
- Bake at 425° for 15 minutes, reduce heat to 350° and continue baking 35-40 minutes.
- If knife test comes out mostly clean, it's done.
- Enjoy this with *your* favorite "punkin!"
- Optional topping: whipped cream with a sprinkle of cinnamon.

YOUR MEMORIES

_____

_____

_____

_____

Traditional Pizza

BY JENNIFER ELWOOD

The Story behind the recipe:

Every year leading up to the holiday season, I plan an event for my family called "Staycation." This event is the epitome of our Bible verse, a wonderful and pleasant practice of living in harmony that adds loving ingredients to the recipe we call "family." And the good news is we don't have to spend a lot or stress out with a lot of packing or preparations!

The week before, we decorate the house, prepare our favorite meals and treats, and when Friday evening arrives, we open new PJs and settle in. We always plan yummy food—including homemade pizza. My kids use such creativity to shape their individual pizzas. As you prepare this fun meal, take some time to enjoy each other's presence and point out the unique beauty that you see God shaping in the lives of your children.

"HOW WONDERFUL IT IS, HOW PLEASANT, FOR GOD'S PEOPLE TO LIVE TOGETHER IN HARMONY!"
–PSALM 133:1 (GNT)

Traditional Pizza

"We love because he first loved us" (1 John 4:19, NIV).

INGREDIENTS

4 cups bread flour
1 1/2 cup warm water
1 envelope or 2 1/2 tsp. instant dry yeast
1 tsp. sugar
2 tsp. kosher salt
2 tsp. vegetable oil, plus a little
to coat the bowl

DIRECTIONS

- Combine dry ingredients in a mixer. Slowly add the wet ingredients. Mix with dough hook 5 minutes or knead for 10.
- Grease bowl with 2 tsp. oil, put dough inside, and cover. Place in a warm spot and rise 1 hour.
- When dough is ready, preheat to 500° with baking sheets in the oven.
- Place each creation on parchment paper to transfer to the hot pan. Use fingertips to gently stretch dough into the desired shape. Top as desired.
- Carefully place your pizzas on the pans and return to the oven. Check at 8 minutes for small pizzas, 12-14 minutes for larger. Use a potholder to lift pizza and check for a fully baked crust.
- Buon appetito!

YOUR MEMORIES

Winter Recipes

"Both day and night belong to you; you made the starlight and the sun. You set the boundaries of the earth, and you made both summer and winter."
(Psalm 74:16-17, NLT)

Wintertime can be filled with wonder, even as the outside around us lies dormant. Cozying up next to a fire or a warm oven can relieve us of winter's chill. A pot of soup and baked goods help to keep tummies happy as we are inside a bit more.

And since the frigid days keep little ones under foot more with a potential case of cabin fever, winter is a perfect time to make some culinary creations with your children. Don't miss the opportunity to draw closer to one another. Family can all be home sequestered in their own respective corners, or they can be interacting. There is surely time for both, but memories are made when we intentionally create together. Have fun with these recipes inspired by the winter season!

Angel Food Cake

BY DENISE PASS

The Story behind the recipe:

As the first light of morning shone through the windows on Christmas day, I knew time was short to finish wrapping gifts. For years, I struggled to help my children see the wonder of Christmas beyond the presents. I wanted Christ to be central to our celebration but honestly, it was hard to do with the busyness that surrounds this special holiday. But it was food that helped me to remind my children of what Christ had done on our behalf. My kids knew and looked forward to the birthday cake I would make for Jesus—that they could eat for breakfast! I chose an angel food cake (seemed fitting); and whipped cream, because He made us as white as snow. Strawberries represented His blood shed on our behalf. I wanted my kids to understand that the gift of Christ coming was so He could lay down His life for us. We sang happy birthday to Jesus and thanked Him for the gifts He gave us in Him. The precious memories made on Christmas day lasted far longer than the gifts we would likely end up returning, anyway.

"FOR GOD SO LOVED THE WORLD, THAT HE GAVE HIS ONLY SON,
THAT WHOEVER BELIEVES IN HIM SHOULD NOT PERISH BUT HAVE ETERNAL LIFE."
–JOHN 3:16 (ESV)

Angel Food Cake

"For everyone who has been born of God overcomes the world.
And this is the victory that has overcome the world—our faith" (1 John 5:4, ESV).

INGREDIENTS

1 1/2 cups egg whites, room temperature, from
10-11 large eggs (or egg whites in carton)
3/4 cup gluten-free, all-purpose flour
1/2 cup cornstarch
3/4 cup powdered sugar
3/4 cup and 2 Tbs. granulated sugar
1/4 tsp. salt
1 1/2 tsp. cream of tartar
1 Tbs. vanilla
1/4 tsp. butter or almond extract

*Regular flour can be substituted for this gluten-free recipe.

DIRECTIONS

- Preheat the oven to 350°.
- Mix flour, cornstarch, and powdered sugar. Set aside.
- Beat egg whites on high until starting to foam then add the salt and cream of tartar.
- Add extract and continue whipping.
- Add granulated sugar slowly to the egg whites while they are whipping until stiff peaks form.
- Slowly fold in dry ingredients with a spatula. Scoop into an ungreased 10-inch round pan.
- Bake at 350° for about 35-40 minutes until a light golden brown. Invert pan right away onto a cooling rack. Cool completely then run a knife along the edges of the pan and carefully plate the cake.

YOUR MEMORIES

Chewy Chocolate Butter Bars

BY ANNE MCCABE

The Story behind the recipe:

There is something about favorite dishes we make over and over again. Our family feels cherished when we make it for them. This was one such recipe for me—made annually by my family for Christmas. It is delicious and provides a wonderful combination of ingredients. I enjoyed making it every year with my mom. The base of the cookie includes a crunchy cereal with sweet and buttery flavors. The topping is a classic favorite. . . melted chocolate! The sweetness poured out on this delicious cookie bar reminds me of how the Lord poured out His sweet Spirit upon mankind. True joy is found in pouring our lives back out for Him. Ask your family what their favorite dishes are and make a point of making it for them. The sweet thoughtfulness in doing so will be a sweet memory that is cherished for a lifetime.

"IN THE LAST DAYS, GOD SAYS, 'I WILL POUR OUT MY SPIRIT UPON ALL PEOPLE. YOUR SONS AND DAUGHTERS WILL PROPHESY. YOUR YOUNG MEN WILL SEE VISIONS, AND YOUR OLD MEN WILL DREAM DREAMS.'"
-ACTS 2:17 (NLT)

Chewy Chocolate Butter Bars

"Even if I am to be poured out as a drink offering upon the sacrificial offering of your faith, I am glad and rejoice with you all" (Philippians 2:17, ESV).

INGREDIENTS

1 cup light corn syrup
1 cup sugar
1 cup peanut butter
1 pkg. 16 oz butterscotch morsels
1 pkg. 16 oz. chocolate morsels
6 cups of preferred rice/corn flakes cereal

DIRECTIONS

- Bring sugar and corn syrup to a boil.
- Turn off the heat and add the peanut butter. Stir until smooth.
- Mix in cereal and stir until completely covered.
- Press into a greased, 13 x 9 baking dish and allow to cool.
- Melt the morsels in a double boiler or very low heat. While stirring, spread on top of the cereal mixture.
- Cool and cut into bite-sized pieces.
- Take to a gathering and enjoy!

YOUR MEMORIES

Christmas Morning Sausage Balls

BY LISA MAPLES

The Story behind the recipe:

On Christmas morning, my family loves to open presents together. My husband and I, with our parents who spend the night on Christmas Eve, sip coffee while the children explore their gifts around the Christmas tree. After a while, one of us goes to the refrigerator to retrieve the sausage balls from the previous night's dinner, heats them up, and delivers them around the Christmas tree. They make the perfect breakfast on Christmas morning as an easy finger food with no mess or utensils needed. Instead of creating an elaborate breakfast, we can focus on the true meaning of Christmas day: Jesus! The sausage balls can be made ahead with the kids' help and stored in the refrigerator a few days in advance of Christmas day. Though this is a perfect Christmas morning dish, we confess to making them all year long!

"AND THIS WILL BE A SIGN FOR YOU: YOU WILL FIND A BABY
WRAPPED IN SWADDLING CLOTHS AND LYING IN A MANGER."
-LUKE 2:12 (ESV)

Christmas Morning Sausage Balls

"Taste and see that the LORD is good; blessed is the one who takes refuge in him" (Psalm 34:8, NIV).

INGREDIENTS

1-pound breakfast sausage, room temp
1 cup finely grated cheddar cheese, room temp
3 cups Bisquick or biscuit mix
2 Tbs. water

Optional ingredients: add 1/2-pound chopped bacon and/or parsley for a festive color addition.

DIRECTIONS

- Preheat the oven to 350°.
- Cover cookie sheet with nonstick cooking spray or parchment paper.
- Combine sausage and cheese with clean hands.
- Add 3 cups Bisquick and water, mix well.
- Roll into small balls and place on baking sheet.
- Bake at 350° for 15-20 minutes.
- Serve or store in an airtight container.
- Enjoy as an appetizer or for breakfast!

YOUR MEMORIES

Dutch Chocolate Snow Ice Cream

BY DENISE PASS

The Story behind the recipe:

There is something about the excitement of snow that brings us back to the simple things and back to the joy of childhood . . . carefree moments where we forget the stress and busyness of life. Whenever it would snow when my kids were growing up, there was excitement because it meant we would have a break from our normal routine. We make special moments when we hit pause on our busy lives every now and then. As we took time to play in the snow, it seemed like the world stopped for a moment. We gathered snow, brought it inside with abounding giggles and eyes widened with wonder as we made ice cream from snow! This recipe, and the sign of snow, are reminders to rest. Even in snow, God has purposes beyond our understanding. And the good news is that we don't have to wait for snow to create this yummy treat. Blend some ice into a crushed ice texture or use a snow cone machine and voila! Homemade snow!

"FOR AS THE RAIN AND THE SNOW COME DOWN FROM HEAVEN AND DO NOT RETURN THERE BUT WATER THE EARTH, MAKING IT BRING FORTH AND SPROUT, GIVING SEED TO THE SOWER AND BREAD TO THE EATER, SO SHALL MY WORD BE THAT GOES OUT FROM MY MOUTH: IT SHALL NOT RETURN TO ME EMPTY, BUT IT SHALL ACCOMPLISH THAT WHICH I PURPOSE, AND SHALL SUCCEED IN THE THING FOR WHICH I SENT IT."
–ISAIAH 55:10-11 (ESV)

Dutch Chocolate Snow Ice Cream

"God thunders wondrously with His voice, doing great things which we do not comprehend. For to the snow He says, 'Fall on the earth,' and to the downpour and the rain, 'Be strong.' He seals the hand of every person, so that all people may know His work" (Job 37:5-7, NASB).

INGREDIENTS

6-8 cups snow*
1 cup heavy whipping cream
1/4 cup sugar (or sugar substitute)
1 1/2 Tbs. cocoa powder
1 pinch of salt
1 tsp. vanilla
1 tsp. butter extract

* Based on texture of snow, add more or less to achieve the consistency you like.

DIRECTIONS

- As everyone knows, hunt for the pure white snow that has not been tinkled on by any critters or the family dog—or make you own in the blender.
- In a large bowl, mix together all of the ingredients except for the snow.
- Incorporate the snow, adding a few cups at a time and whisking together ingredients.
- Pack the snow into a cup and scoop it out. Enjoy!
- Other add-ins: For Rocky Road ice cream, add marshmallow cream and walnuts. For Chocolate mint, add a tsp. of mint extract.

YOUR MEMORIES

_____
_____
_____
_____

Homemade Soft Pretzels

BY DENISE PASS

The Story behind the recipe:

Hunger is an indicator of our need. We long to get it filled. And when we take extra care to delight our loved one's tastebuds, we create a memory. But don't let that hunger go to waste. As we feed and nurture our families, we want them to see a greater hunger that only God will fully satisfy. Creating fun meals, snacks, or desserts is foundational to helping our children see God's provision as more than just filling our hunger. Food brings opportunities for fellowship and stimulating conversation about the things of God. And the atmosphere we create surrounding the food we create matters, too. I love this recipe because it was hands on for everyone and no one was left out. Watching my children engage in the project and with one another was a beautiful memory that I will cherish always. This recipe satisfied my tribe in so many ways. We had fun making the pretzels and the taste was amazing. When my daughter was diagnosed with Celiac Disease in 2002, we thought our baking days were over. Thank God that was not the case with these gluten free wonders!

"BLESSED ARE THOSE WHO HUNGER AND THIRST FOR RIGHTEOUSNESS, FOR THEY SHALL BE SATISFIED."
—MATTHEW 5:6 (ESV)

Homemade Soft Pretzels

"So, whether you eat or drink, or whatever you do, do all to the glory of God" (1 Corinthians 10:31, ESV).

INGREDIENTS

Pretzels:
3 cups gluten-free flour (or reg. flour)
1 ½ tsp. xanthan gum (none if using reg. flour)
1 Tbs. instant yeast
1/4 tsp. cream of tartar
1/4 tsp. baking soda
2 Tbsp. light brown sugar
1 tsp. salt
2 Tbsp. butter, melted
1 large egg
1 ¼ cup water
Baking soda bath: (after pretzels are shaped)
1/2 cup baking soda, 9 cups boiling water

DIRECTIONS

- Mix the dry ingredients. Add wet ingredients.
- Knead dough in mixer until no longer sticking.
- Place dough in bowl, cover, let rise 1 hour.
- Divide dough into 8 equal balls.
- Line baking sheets with parchment paper.
- Roll each ball into a thin rope, 12-inches long. Make a circle with the dough and twist ends together. Bring the twisted ends back down towards yourself and press them down to form a pretzel shape. Let rise for 15-20 minutes.
- Drop pretzels into baking soda bath. Let boil for 20-30 seconds, place onto baking sheet.
- Brush with butter and sprinkle on coarse salt.
- Bake at 400° for 12-15 minutes, or until done.

YOUR MEMORIES

Jesus the Cornerstone Gingerbread House

Special thanks to Jennifer Elwood for making this recipe & for the photo!

BY JENNIFER ELWOOD

The Story behind the recipe:

Making a gingerbread house from scratch is a brand-new tradition for our family. When creating recipes to accompany a Christmas devotional I wrote, we needed a gingerbread house to photograph. . . in July. Since there were none in the store, we had to make our own. The aroma that enveloped the kitchen as cinnamon, ginger, and molasses mingled was heavenly and convinced me to never purchase one in a box again! As a family, we've enjoyed creating gingerbread house masterpieces for years. That year, however, we added Jesus as the cornerstone. Sometimes we get so wrapped up in Jesus the baby we forget that He grew up and revealed Himself as our Messiah, fully God and fully man. Intentionally adding Jesus as the cornerstone to our Christmas creations helps represent the true reason for Christmas. And bonus––it's the perfect holiday season conversation starter!

"THE STONE THAT THE BUILDERS REJECTED HAS BECOME THE CORNERSTONE. THIS IS THE LORD'S DOING;
IT IS MARVELOUS IN OUR EYES."
–PSALM 118:22-23 (ESV)

Jesus The Cornerstone Gingerbread House

"As it is written: 'See, I lay in Zion a stone that causes people to stumble and a rock that makes them fall, and the one who believes in him will never be put to shame'" (Romans 9:33, NIV).

INGREDIENTS

2 cups granulated white sugar
1 cup plus 2 Tbs. brown sugar
1 cup solid vegetable oil (or butter)
4 eggs
3 Tbs. molasses
1 1/4 tsp. salt
2 tsp. baking soda
1 Tbs. ginger
1 Tbs. cinnamon
6 cups flour
For decorating: Royal icing (4 cups egg whites and 4 cups confectioners' sugar beaten well, use before it dries out), candies of choice, small toy to represent Jesus.

DIRECTIONS

- Put shortening and sugar in mixer and combine. Add one egg at a time, mix until fluffy.
- Add molasses, ginger, cinnamon, salt, and baking soda, beat until well incorporated.
- Add the flour slowly, dough will be stiff.
- Roll out to 1/4-inch thickness, use a printed template, cut out the shapes and Jesus corner.
- Cover baking sheets in parchment and bake at 375° for 10-12 minutes. Let cool completely.
- Pipe royal icing (or hot glue, I won't tell!) Allow to set fully.
- Decorate with remaining icing, candies, and Jesus figure. Share your creation with the world!

YOUR MEMORIES

Melt-In-Your-Mouth Molasses Cookies

BY DANIELLE POORMAN

The Story behind the recipe:

Cookies are a staple favorite not just during the holidays, but all year round. When I was a little girl, my Nana baked the most amazing, delicious molasses cookies. We'd consume them in fluffy rounds or roll them out and make cookies for the Christmas season. There was nothing like my Nana's soft, melt-in-your-mouth molasses cookies. It was the unique spice in the cookies that made it so delicious.

Now that my children are older, they love being in the kitchen with me. Whether we're cooking or baking, it's always a treat to share my childhood recipe memories with them. As recipes are passed down, more than just eating and fellowship happens. We are doing life together. Getting hands-on in the kitchen is one of our favorite times to talk and share life together.

"HE WHO GIVES FOOD TO ALL FLESH, FOR HIS STEADFAST LOVE ENDURED FOREVER."
–1 THESSALONIANS 2:15 (ESV)

Melt-In-Your-Mouth Molasses Cookies

"The Lord is good to those who wait for him, to the soul who seeks him" (Lamentations 3:25, ESV).

INGREDIENTS

1 cup sugar
1 cup shortening (melted)
1 cup molasses
1 egg
4 tsp. baking soda
2/3 cup hot water
1 1/2 tsp. cream of tartar
1 1/2 tsp. ground ginger
1 1/2 tsp. ground cinnamon
1/2 tsp. ground cloves
3/4 tsp. salt
5 cups white flour
1 Tbs. vanilla

DIRECTIONS

- Preheat oven to 400°.
- In large bowl, sift together dry ingredients: cream of tartar, ginger, cinnamon, cloves, salt, and flour. Mix gently and set aside.
- Melt shortening and let cool. Mix cooled shortening, sugar, molasses, add egg, and mix.
- Dissolve baking soda into hot water. Add to wet mixture. Add vanilla and dry ingredients. Mix well.
- Place in fridge for 20 minutes.
- Remove bowl and roll dough to 1/8-inch thickness on lightly floured surface.
- Cut out rounds with cookie cutter and place on a lightly greased pan.
- Bake about 10 minutes until lightly brown. They should still be soft to touch. Let cool and enjoy!

YOUR MEMORIES

69

Savory Egg Casserole

BY DENISE PASS

The Story behind the recipe:

One thing I loved to do when an event or a holiday was coming up was to make most of the food ahead of time so I could enjoy and savor the moments with my people. Egg casserole was a favorite and this recipe is a conglomeration of our favorite ingredients. Truly I would use what we had on hand. But making this the day before meant I could enjoy a cup of coffee and conversation with family and friends, rather than slaving in the kitchen.

This recipe reminds me of the intentionality that blesses our family in our role as mommas. I had to plan to make sure we had devotion time, and believe me, we also missed plenty. Every time I would get my schedule the way I liked it; something would change. But persevering through all the twists and turns, I would put another schedule on the fridge. Just because we don't execute our plan perfectly does not mean our planning will not bear fruit. Plan ahead so you can enjoy those around you more as you do life together.

"GOOD PLANNING AND HARD WORK LEAD TO PROSPERITY, BUT HASTY SHORTCUTS LEAD TO POVERTY."
-PROVERBS 21:5 (NLT)

Savory Egg Casserole

"The heart of man plans his way, but the Lord establishes his steps" (Proverbs 16:9, ESV).

INGREDIENTS

5-pound bag of potatoes
1 onion
2 cloves garlic
1 red pepper
1 green pepper
2 cups spinach
1/2-pound bacon, cooked
10 eggs
8 oz. shredded mild cheddar cheese

Optional: add 1/2 roll sausage or substitute for bacon

DIRECTIONS

- Preheat oven to 350°.
- Cook bacon in deep pan, set aside on paper towel.
- If use turkey bacon, then use a couple Tbsp. oil.
- Cook potatoes in a couple Tbsp. bacon grease.
- Add vegetables and cook until tender.
- Pour potatoes and vegetables in a glass dish coated with non-stick spray.
- Sprinkle grated cheese on top.
- Beat eggs in bowl and pour atop of cheese.
- Cut bacon into pieces and sprinkle on top.
- Bake for 30-40 minutes, testing to see if it is complete.

YOUR MEMORIES

Mommy & Me: Meet the Contributors

FROM THE SEEING DEEP TEAM

The Beauty of Adoption

Jennifer with daughters (left to right), Ella, Holly, and Carol—photo credits Angie Waddle

BY JENNIFER ELWOOD

"BUT WHEN THE RIGHT TIME CAME, GOD SENT HIS SON, BORN OF A WOMAN, SUBJECT TO LAW. GOD SENT HIM TO BUY FREEDOM FOR US WHO WERE SLAVES TO THE LAW, SO THAT HE COULD ADOPT US AS HIS VERY OWN CHILDREN" (GALATIANS 4:4-5, NLT).

Adoption is a part of our story that takes center stage. All three of my daughters entered my family through the miracle of adoption. When meeting new people, I often write my unusual family tree on a napkin or scrap of paper because with so many moving parts, it's hard to keep track of all the extended family relationships we navigate every day.

My family owns Taste and See Deli Bakery, managed by my bonus daughter Holly. We regularly talk about food or hang out in the kitchen; it is the center of our interactions and truly is a highlight of my life. Carol, Ella and I often come when there's new creations to try, which means I'm blessed to watch three of my hearts love on each other regularly. Sometimes, I can scarcely believe the blessing I've received through such beautiful daughters and the amazing, unique way God brought them all into my life. This revelation often comes to mind as we eat together, dream about new deli treats, and enjoy each other's company.

Mamas, we don't need to look far into scripture to see that our Father God has a special place in his heart for adoption that applies to all of us. Everyone who has put their faith in Jesus *are* adopted. Jesus made a way for us all to be a part of God's family. He voluntarily died, defeated death, and rose again—simply to bring us home. Our faultless, sinless adoption broker patiently awaits to deliver all who believe in Him safely to their true Father.

All Things Work Together for Good

Robin and daughter, Alana—photo credits Jim Gerblick

BY ROBIN GERBLICK

"HE EXISTED BEFORE ANYTHING ELSE, AND HE HOLDS ALL CREATION" (COLOSSIANS 1:7, NLT).

The kitchen has always been the heart and hub of our family traditions but ever since I can remember, our "kitchen" was located in the great outdoors. My parents wanted us to experience all of God's creation in nature so camping and boating trips became our training ground. From bacon and eggs over an open campfire, to delicacies like Spam and pineapple topped with brown sugar, wrapped in foil and placed on top of open coals, we became back-country chefs in the making.

Last summer, my daughter and I decided to take our outdoor cuisine to the next level and master Dutch oven cooking. It's a complicated and precise activity, but we worked seamlessly together trusting that Jesus works *all* things together for His good! The words of our experiences additionally ring true in Ecclesiastes 4:17, "Two are better than one, because they have a good return for their labor." (NIV)

The real lessons over the years came from what we learned as a family; working together, honoring our unique gifts and loving each other unconditionally as we navigated uncharted waters, deserts and mountains, each posing an element of adventure and trust. Just like Jesus who loves and cares for us through every circumstance and trial, my family was there to support and encourage. Now that we have children and grandchildren, those lessons are priceless. Teaching the next generation about the great adventure of loving Jesus, and how His love never leaves us, is a lesson enhanced in the beauty of the great outdoors.

Promise Keeper

Tabatha and her son, Gabriel—photo credits Brandy Christine Photography

BY TABATHA HAINES

"SO AFTER WAITING PATIENTLY, ABRAHAM RECEIVED WHAT WAS PROMISED" (HEBREWS 6:15, NIV).

Thirteen. It's the number of years my husband and I prayed before we received our long-awaited son. Having our Miracle Boy taught me that when God makes a promise to you, He is faithful to keep it, even if it takes longer than expected.

Sometimes, that promise was the only thing I could cling to when my house lay quiet and belly flat. My faith was like a small mustard seed grown in soil plowed by patience, watered by tears, and tended with empty hands lifted in praise, until the day that my arms were filled with God's faithfulness. Filled with a beautiful newborn baby boy.

I've had three years to look, laugh, and enjoy my promise. I love to tell the story of how he got here. He is quick to hug and even quicker to help me, especially in the kitchen. I have never been a great cook or baker for that matter. I seem to have a real knack for poor measuring and burning things but having that little guy with me makes the task much more enjoyable.

We laugh, learn, talk, cook, and when he's big enough to understand, I'll share his own story with him. A story of hope, endurance and promise, and I pray that one day he will call God his own Faithful Friend and Promise Keeper. Can you recall a time in your life when God was faithful to keep His promise to you? If so, share your story with someone today. It might just grow their faith, too!

Tonna, granddaughter Henli, and daughter Kensi

BY TONNA LOGAN

"LO, CHILDREN *ARE* A HERITAGE OF THE LORD: *AND* THE FRUIT OF THE WOMB *IS HIS* REWARD"
(PSALM 127:3, KJV).

Although my five children are now grown, I cherish the memories of the quality time we have spent together through the years. Each one special and significant in their own unique way in my heart and each one has a favorite dish that I cook. These personal preferences are continued year after year when we gather for holidays, birthdays, and other special occasions. I always know what to prepare because of their love of a certain recipe with my secret ingredients added. I will sometimes tell them the particular ingredient that makes the recipe so yummy. Truthfully though, it is also the love and patience added with just the right measure of the Lord's help that yields a fruitful, blue-ribbon outcome every time.

My children now have their own families, which means extended family members call me with requests to make particular foods or ask for the recipe. When someone delves into one of my tried-and-true recipes, we gladly compare with satisfying goodness. I am now also able to watch and teach my grandchildren in the kitchen and it could not be more rewarding. They prepare and are so proud of their own creations when they serve their finished dishes.

Our Lord knows exactly what He is doing. It continues to make me feel loved and needed just knowing that creating delicious food is something they are still fond of. The dishes we create for loved one's bear fruit for years to come.

Cultivating Fruit-filled Traditions

Grace and Hannah (left to right) with their mom, Lisa

BY LISA MAPLES

"BUT THE FRUIT OF THE SPIRIT IS LOVE, JOY, PEACE, PATIENCE, KINDNESS, GOODNESS, FAITHFULNESS, GENTLENESS, SELF-CONTROL; AGAINS SUCH THINGS THERE IS NO LAW" (GALATIANS 5:22-23, ESV).

Every summer, my family travels to the beach to dip our toes in the surf and unwind in the ocean breezes. We treasure memories of our daughters happily skipping with sandcastle buckets to our beach tent where they would create their dream castles. They love building these masterpieces!

While shopping one day, I discovered a Bundt cake pan in the shape of a castle and immediately connected it with the sandcastle molds that occupied my kids for hours at the ocean. Little did I know, baking a cake at the beach would become a beloved, nostalgic family tradition each summer. We enjoy baking and decorating our edible, beach-inspired masterpiece as much as building its sandy counterpart.

The process of creating a cake is a training exercise of taking turns, considering the feelings of others, embracing the creative process, and enjoying the final product. Annually baking this sandcastle cake has cultivated the traits of joy, patience, kindness and gentleness in my children. Tradition sets expectations for how we love each other and enjoy our precious time together.

One day, our children will have the responsibility of mixing the right amounts of love, joy, peace, patience, kindness, goodness, faithfulness, gentleness, and self-control into their homes. I'm glad that God inspires us, even while creating in the kitchen, to develop just the right conditions to train our children and allow His fruit to grow in them.

Beautiful Timing

Anne and her daughter, BeccaJoy—photo credits Jeff Pokorny

BY ANNE MCCABE

"FOR EVERYTHING THERE IS A SEASON, AND A TIME FOR EVERY MATTER UNDER HEAVEN. HE HAS MADE EVERYTHING BEAUTIFUL IN HIS TIME" (ECCLESIASTES 3:1, 11, ESV).

The arrival of my first two daughters came as beautiful blessings in my thirties and then . . . surprise! My third daughter arrived in my mid-forties. She was surely God's idea and suited His timing, not mine. When my fear of our challenging circumstances at the time overwhelmed me, the Lord spoke this to my heart, "This baby will 'beckon joy' into all of your lives." My firstborn's chosen name for her was embraced: BeccaJoy.

God loves to shake things up like a well-balanced, tossed salad because He knows, in His time, what is good for us! BeccaJoy's infectious grin coupled with bold beauty, in her red ringlets and the way her spirit danced joyfully around each one of us, was what each family member needed to navigate through the trying circumstances that followed her birth.

Timing is important in the kitchen. Baked goods can be ruined with just a minute too long in the oven. A recipe provides direction that guides us to better results. God gives us His Word as the perfect recipe book to guide us. We are wise to depend on His Word and trust His beautiful timing even when we may not understand. When we do, hearts can be wonderfully drawn together with laughter and grace, as in our family with BeccaJoy, at just the right time.

Discipleship in the Daily

Denise and her family—December 2020

BY DENISE PASS

"WHATEVER YOU DO, WORK AT IT WITH ALL YOUR HEART, AS WORKING FOR THE LORD . . . IT IS THE LORD CHRIST YOU ARE SERVING" (COLOSSIANS 3:23-24, NIV).

Dragging a wagon full of cookies, with cold tiny fingers carrying the violins and guitar, my tribe and I made our annual rounds to carol to ALL of the neighbors in our development. There were times when we made a meal for someone going through a difficult time. At other times, we would sing at nursing homes and share the gift of worship along with some snacks that were lovingly made or purchased. Their help made the difference as we served together! We cherish those we serve food to, and sometimes this opens the door to share Christ.

Food is a big part of our lives and daily interaction with loved ones. Moms, we have an opportunity with hospitality to nurture our families, entertain strangers, and perhaps even angels. While meal preparation can become a tedious occupation, when we remember that whatever we do is for the LORD, it is worthwhile and will bear fruit. And when we consider that food can be used to share the Gospel with others and also create space for fellowship, we see hospitality as the gift it is.

All the years have flown by so quickly, friends. What precious memories I have! Helping my kids know the truth and the One Who lovingly created them was the singular most important thing to me. Faith was infused in all we did—in our education, our service in the church, even in our cooking. Friends, the discipleship of our children is continually changing throughout the seasons of our lives. It is in the daily—moment by moment. Carpe Diem!

Embracing Grace Through Our Messy Moments

Chloe, mom Danielle, and Calvin—photo credits Chad Poorman

BY DANIELLE POORMAN

"BUT HE SAID TO ME, 'MY GRACE IS SUFFICIENT FOR YOU, FOR MY POWER IS MADE PERFECT IN WEAKNESS.' THEREFORE, I WILL BOAST ALL THE MORE GLADLY OF MY WEAKNESS, SO THAT THE POWER OF CHRIST MAY REST ON ME" (2 CORINTHIANS 12:9, ESV).

Motherhood comes with many challenges including remaining present with our families. Feeling the pull in many directions leaves us overwhelmed and exhausted. Endless dishes, diapers, and laundry claim so much of our time and energy we often feel like we have nothing left to give.

What if we paused the pile(s) of laundry and dishes for a moment or two? Consider leaving the clutter for a bit to cherish snuggles, favorite stories, or get a little messy in the kitchen together. The kitchen is one of my favorite places to create. Floured fingers and sticky faces produce smiles and delight. Pausing to prioritize creation over clutter, while engaging in small things, writes an important message on the hearts of our children. God's grace abounds in every moment.

If you're like me, embracing these messy moments may require some practice. Although we can feel distracted by the mess, it's in these messy moments that we experience grace and joy. They are the perfect canvas for God's grace. Living fully present in these moments allows us to realize we're covered in grace and we can cherish this beautiful gift of motherhood. Uniquely made in the image of Almighty God, our messy moments reveal the way He orchestrates the details in our joy and sorrow. Regardless of how our lives look, we can embrace everyday moments with our children. We can savor the moments, big and small, especially in our messy kitchens.

Thank you for joining us in this sacred space where moms work beside their children in the kitchen imparting faith and life lessons. We have created some space in here for you to jot notes to loved ones—memories or recipe tweaks, what have you. Maybe there are some moments you don't want to forget, or a tip you don't want to leave out. Have fun creating together and remember that time in the kitchen is treasured time. Here are seven tips to help remind us of what matters most.

Tip #1: Love your people well. Don't let the little stuff get in the way of relationship. "Above all, keep loving one another earnestly, since love covers a multitude of sins" (1 Peter 4:8, ESV).

Tip #2: Mix in lots of sugar into your daily lives. Encourage one another, but don't sugar coat. "How sweet are your words to my taste, sweeter than honey to my mouth" (Psalm 109:103)!

Tip #3: Don't let messes ruin your day. Laughter has a way of cleaning up the mess on the inside so the mess on the outside does not matter as much. "He will yet fill your mouth with laughter, and your lips with shouting" (Job 8:21, ESV).

Tip #4: Don't take yourself too seriously but seriously apply faith to all of life. "Now faith is the assurance of things hoped for, the conviction of things not seen" (Hebrews 11:1, ESV).

Tip #5: Don't be afraid to try new things; don't get boxed in by the demands of life. "But the fruit of the Spirit is love, joy, peace, patience, kindness, goodness, faithfulness" (Galatians 5:22, ESV).

Tip #6: Have people over. Even if you don't feel like hospitality is your gift. "Show hospitality to one another without grumbling" (1 Peter 4:9).

Tip #7: Don't do all the cooking. Include others and watch your relationship grow! "Two are better than one, because they have a good reward for their toil" (Ecclesiastes 4:9, ESV).

Scriptures to Encourage You

Proverbs 31:25-30 ESV
"Strength and dignity are her clothing, and she laughs at the time to come. She opens her mouth with wisdom, and the teaching of kindness is on her tongue. She looks well to the ways of her household and does not eat the bread of idleness. Her children rise up and call her blessed; her husband also, and he praises her: "Many women have done excellently, but you surpass them all.""

Proverbs 31:26-27 ESV
"She opens her mouth with wisdom, and the teaching of kindness is on her tongue. She looks well to the ways of her household and does not eat the bread of idleness."

Proverbs 22:6 ESV
"Train up a child in the way he should go; even when he is old he will not depart from it."

Psalm 127:3 ESV
"Behold, children are a heritage from the Lord, the fruit of the womb a reward."

Proverbs 23:22-25 ESV
"Listen to your father who gave you life, and do not despise your mother when she is old. Buy truth, and do not sell it; buy wisdom, instruction, and understanding. The father of the righteous will greatly rejoice; he who fathers a wise son will be glad in him. Let your father and mother be glad; let her who bore you rejoice."

Ephesians 6:2 ESV
"Honor your father and mother" (this is the first commandment with a promise)."

2 Timothy 1:5 ESV
"I am reminded of your sincere faith, a faith that dwelt first in your grandmother Lois and your mother Eunice and now, I am sure, dwells in you as well."

Notes

Notes

Seeing Deep Ministries

If we are honest, life does not measure up to our expectations most of the time. Living in a fallen world, our hearts ache to be with Jesus. Our heart is to encourage you to go deeper into God's word to find the joy that this world has stolen. "Seeing Deep in a Shallow World", we seek to find Christ in all of life and to apply His word so we can "overcome the battles of the mind with the word of God."

We hope your hearts have been encouraged with this little book that is about so much more than cooking. We would love to have you visit with us on our website (www.seeingdeep.com) to see the various resources we offer. Below are a few of the discipleship tools we have for the family, individuals, and churches, including "The Bible Tribe" daily bible reading plan journal, that includes a live 3-minute accompaniment study available on YouTube or via podcast, "31 Days to Hope Reinvented", a devotional and accompaniment study guide to lead you through grief to find hope, and "Shame Off You", which discusses the role shame can play in our lives and how to remove shame biblically. Coming in 2021, a new book release on overcoming mindsets and having the mind of Christ! Original worship music also available on our website. For speaking or worship leading requests, visit our website.

Books

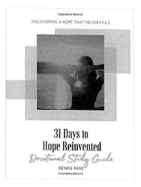

Music & Podcasts

Made in the USA
Middletown, DE
30 September 2021